SCUOLA D'INGLESE
1° livello

The Three Little Pigs
I tre porcellini

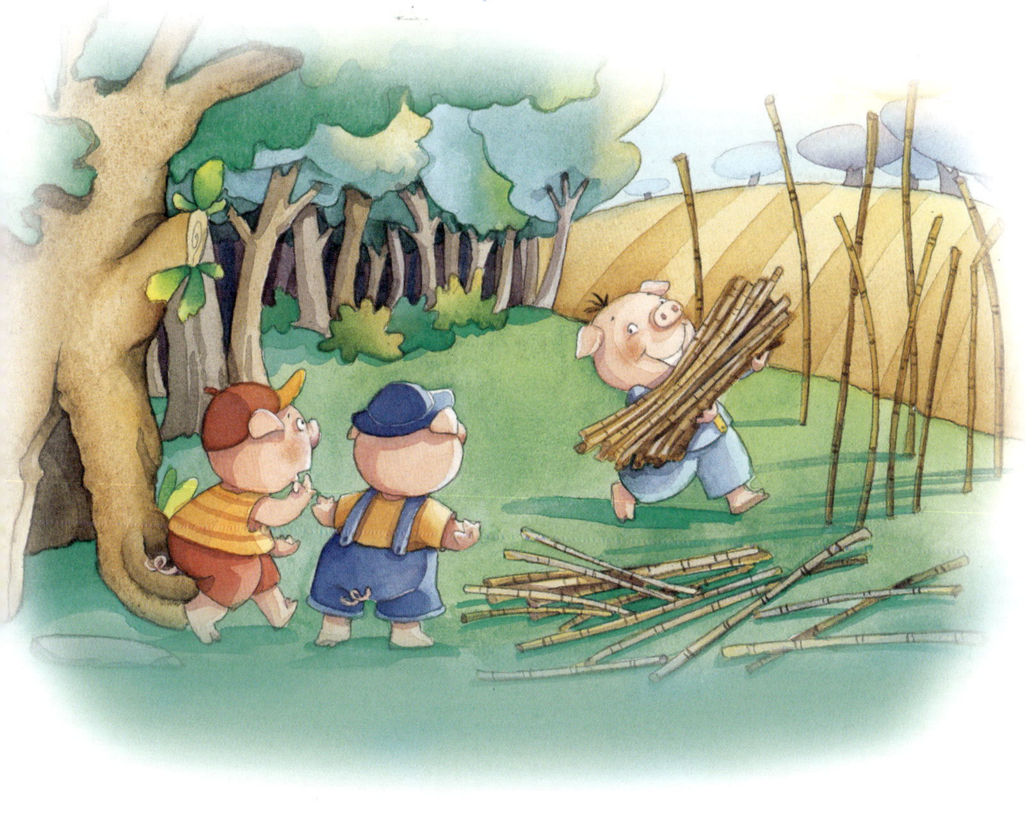

This is the story
of three little pigs.
They live together
with their father
and their mother.

One day Mother Pig says
to her three sons:
– Your father and I
love you very much.
But it's time for you
to leave home.

– We are ready to leave –
answer the three little
pigs.
Mother Pig reminds them
to never let a wolf
in their homes.
– Goodbye, Mum!
– Remember my words,
watch out for the wolf!

The three little pigs walk down the road. They are very happy.

The three little pigs begin
to look for a place
to build their houses.

They meet
a man carrying
some straw.
The first little Pig
decides to buy some.

– I want to build
a house of straw! –
says the first
little Pig.

So he begins to build it.

He likes his house
of straw very much.

The first little Pig
goes inside,
locks the door
and falls asleep.

In the meantime the wolf comes out of his den to look for something to eat.

Suddenly the first little Pig hears a knock at his door.
– Who's there? –
asks the first little Pig.
– A friend – the wolf answers.

The wolf huffs and puffs and he blows the house down. Then he eats the poor little pig in one big gulp!

In the meantime
the second little Pig
and the third little Pig
meet a man selling sticks.
The second little Pig says:
– That's what I want!
A house of sticks!

He works hard to build his house. Then he goes inside, locks the door and falls asleep.

Suddenly he hears
someone knocking
at the door.
KNOCK! KNOCK!
– Who's there? – shouts
the second little Pig.
– I'm your brother – the
wolf says.

The second little Pig doesn't let him in. So the wolf huffs and puffs and blows the house down.

Then the wolf eats the second little Pig in one big gulp.

Now the third little Pig walks down the road alone.

He meets a man
selling bricks.

"That's what
I want!
I want to build
my house with bricks!"
thinks the third little Pig.

Slowly and carefully
the pig builds his house.

He goes inside, locks
the door and lights
a big fire in the fireplace.
Then he puts a large
pot on the fire
to cook
his dinner.

Suddenly he hears someone
knocking at the door.
– Who's there? –
asks the third little Pig.
– Open the door! –
answers the wolf.

– I know who you are! – cries the third little Pig.
– Go away!

– Open the door!
Let me in! –
says the wolf.
– You can't
come in! – answers
the third little Pig.

So the wolf
huffs and puffs
but he can't blow
the house down.

The wolf is very angry.
– Ok little pig,
I'll come down
the chimney!

– You can try
if you want! – says
the third little Pig.
– I'm ready
for you!

The wolf takes a ladder
and he goes up
to the roof.

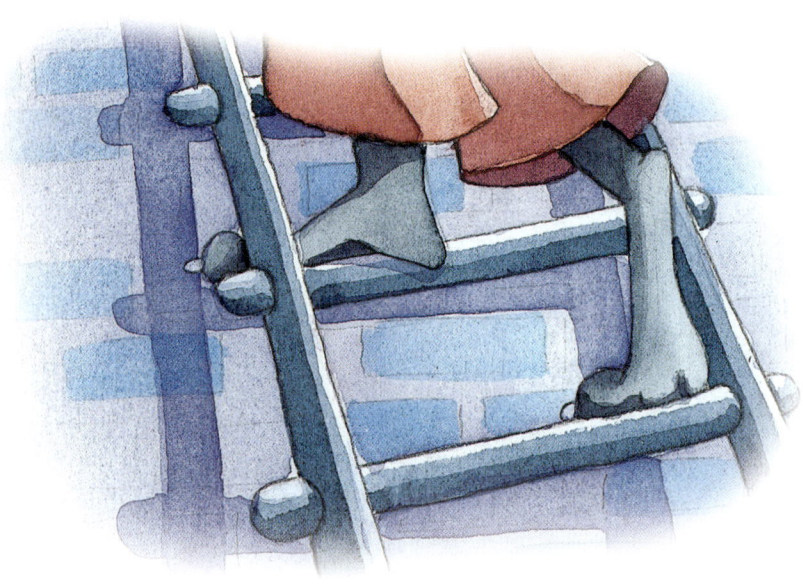

Then he jumps down the chimney and...

... he falls right
into the pot
of boiling water!

And that is the end
of the big bad wolf…

... and the first day
of a new life
for the third little Pig!

TRADUZIONE

INGLESE / ITALIANO

I tre porcellini

Pagina 3
This is the story of three little pigs. They live with their father and their mother.

Questa è la storia di tre porcellini. Vivono con il papà e con la mamma.

Pagina 4
One day Mother Pig says to her three sons:
– Your father and I love you very much. But it's time for you to leave home.

*Un giorno la Mamma dice ai suoi tre figli:
– Vostro padre e io vi amiamo molto. Ma per voi è ora di andare via di casa.*

Pagina 6
– We are ready to leave – answer the three little pigs.
Mother Pig reminds them to never let a wolf in their homes.
– Goodbye, Mum!
– Remember my words, watch out for the wolf!

– Siamo pronti per partire – rispondono i tre porcellini.
La mamma ricorda loro di non lasciare mai entrare un lupo in casa.
– Ciao, mamma!
– Ricordate le mie parole, state attenti al lupo!

Pagina 8
The three little pigs walk down the road.
They are very happy.

I tre porcellini si incamminano per la strada.
Sono molto felici.

Pagina 10
The three little pigs begin to look for a place to build their houses.

I tre porcellini cominciano a cercare un posto per costruire le loro case.

Pagina 12
They meet a man carrying some straw.
The first little Pig decides to buy some.

Incontrano un uomo che trasporta della paglia.
Il primo Porcellino decide di comprarne un po'.

Pagina 13
– I want to build a house of straw - says the first little Pig.

– Voglio costruire una casa di paglia! – dice il primo Porcellino.

Pagina 15
So he begins to build it.

Così inizia a costruirla.

Pagina 16
He likes his house of straw very much.

Gli piace molto la sua casa di paglia.

Pagina 18
The first little Pig goes inside, locks the door and falls asleep.

Il primo Porcellino entra, chiude a chiave la porta e si addormenta.

Pagina 19
In the meantime the wolf comes out of his den to look for something to eat.

Nel frattempo il lupo esce dalla sua tana per cercare qualcosa da mangiare.

Pagina 20
Suddenly the first little Pig hears a knock at his door.
– Who's there? – asks the first little Pig.
– A friend – the wolf answers.

All'improvviso il primo Porcellino sente bussare alla porta.
– Chi è? – chiede il primo Porcellino.
– Un amico – risponde il lupo.

Pagina 21
The wolf huffs and puffs and he blows the house down.
Then he eats the poor little pig in one big gulp!

Il lupo sbuffa e soffia e butta giù la casa. Poi mangia il povero porcellino in un gran boccone!

Pagina 22
In the meantime the second little Pig and the third little Pig meet a man selling sticks. The second little Pig says: – That's what I want! A house of sticks!

Nel frattempo il secondo e il terzo Porcellino incontrano un uomo che vende assicelle di legno. Il secondo Porcellino dice: – Ecco che cosa voglio! Una casa di assicelle!

Pagina 23
He works hard to build his house. Then he goes inside, locks the door and falls asleep.

Lavora duramente per costruire la sua casa. Poi entra, chiude a chiave la porta e si addormenta.

Pagina 24
Suddenly he hears someone knocking at the door.
KNOCK! KNOCK!
– Who's there? – shouts the second little Pig.
– I'm your brother – the wolf says.

*All'improvviso sente qualcuno bussare alla porta. TOC! TOC!
– Chi è? – grida il secondo Porcellino.
– Sono tuo fratello – dice il lupo.*

Pagina 25
The second little Pig doesn't let him in. So the wolf huffs and puffs and he blows the house down.

Il secondo Porcellino non lo lascia entrare. Allora il lupo soffia e sbuffa e butta giù la casa.

Pagina 26
Then the wolf eats the second little Pig in one big gulp.

Poi il lupo mangia il secondo Porcellino in un gran boccone.

Pagina 27
Now the third little Pig walks down the road alone.

Il terzo Porcellino cammina da solo lungo la strada.

Pagina 28
He meets a man selling bricks.

Incontra un uomo che vende mattoni.

Pagina 29
"That's what I want! I want to build my house with bricks!" thinks the third little Pig.

"Ecco ciò che voglio! Voglio costruire la mia casa con i mattoni!" pensa il terzo Porcellino.

Pagina 31
Slowly and carefully the pig builds his house.

Il porcellino costruisce la sua casa lentamente e accuratamente.

Pagina 32
He goes inside, locks the door and lights a big fire in the fireplace. Then he puts a large pot on the fire to cook his dinner.

Entra dentro, chiude a chiave la porta e accende un grande fuoco nel camino. Poi mette una grande pentola sul fuoco per prepararsi la cena.

Pagina 33
Suddenly he hears someone knocking at the door.
– Who's there? – asks the third little Pig.
– Open the door! – answers the wolf.

All'improvviso ente qualcuno bussare alla porta.
– Chi è? – chiede il terzo Porcellino.
– Apri la porta! – risponde il lupo.

Pagina 34
– I know who you are! – cries the third little Pig.
– Go away!

– So chi sei! – esclama il terzo Porcellino.
– Vai via!

Pagina 35
– Open the door! Let me in! – says the wolf.
– You can't come in! – answers the third little Pig.

– *Apri la porta! Fammi entrare! – dice il lupo.*
– *Non puoi entrare! – risponde il terzo Porcellino.*

Pagina 36
So the wolf huffs and puffs but he can't blow the house down.

Allora il lupo sbuffa e soffia, ma non riesce a buttare giù la casa.

Pagina 38
The wolf is very angry.
– Ok little pig, I'll come down the chimney!

Il lupo è molto arrabbiato.
– *Va bene piccolo porcellino, scendo dal camino!*

Pagina 39
–You can try if you want! – says the third little Pig.
– I'm ready for you!

– *Puoi provarci se vuoi – dice il terzo Porcellino.*
– *Sono pronto per te!*

Pagina 40
The wolf takes a ladder and he goes up to the roof.

Il lupo prende una scala e sale sul tetto.

Pagina 41
Then he jumps down the chimney and...

Così il lupo salta giù per il camino e...

Pagina 42
... he falls right into the pot of boiling water!

... cade dritto nella pentola dell'acqua bollente!

Pagina 44
And that is the end of the big bad wolf...

E questa è la fine del grosso lupo cattivo...

Pagina 45
... and the first day of a new life for the third little Pig!

... e il primo giorno di una nuova vita per il terzo Porcellino!

Short summary

There are three .
Their  tells them it is time to leave  and she reminds them about the big bad .
 builds a house of . builds a house of .
And  builds a house of .

The big bad 🐺 blows the 🏠 down, then he eats 🐷; then blows the 🏚 down and eats 🐷. Then the big bad wolf huffs and puffs the 🏠, but the 🏠 is too strong and he can't blow it down. The 🐺 is very angry. So he decides to go down the 🐺 but... he falls into a big 🍲 of hot water!

Find the Differences

Look carefully at the two pictures
and find the five differences.

*Osserva attentamente le due immagini
e trova le cinque differenze.*

A Wordsearch
Find four words of the story!

Trova quattro parole della storia!

PIG **ROAD**
WOLF **HOUSE**

Q	W	G	I	N	L
H	O	U	S	E	Y
Z	L	Y	U	I	Z
B	F	J	I	T	V
R	Y	B	P	I	G
Q	W	S	D	P	G
R	O	A	D	H	J

What is this?
Join the numbers from one to eleven!

Unisci i numeri dall'uno all'undici!

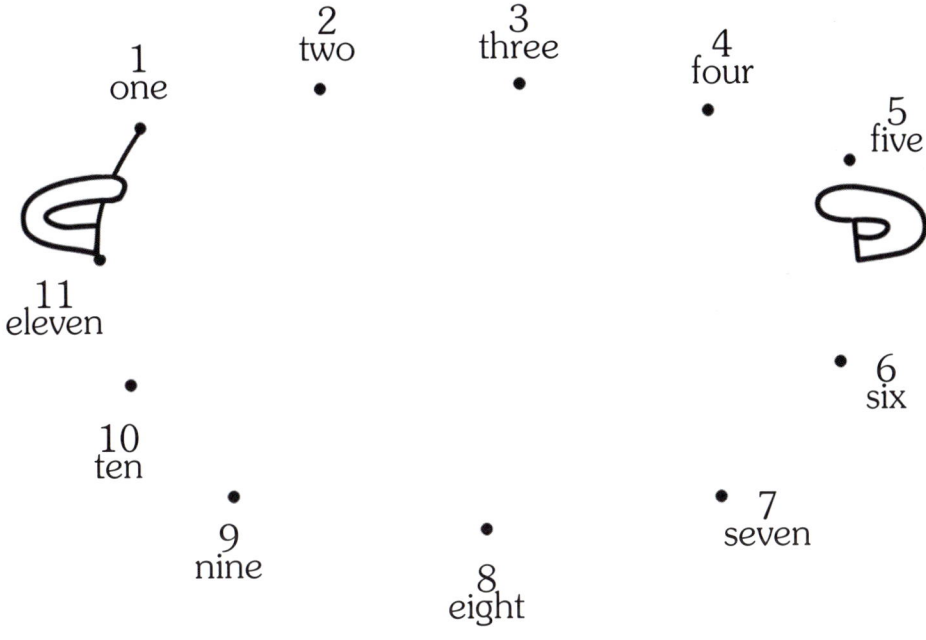

THIS IS A P _ _ !

Match the Word with the picture!

Unisci parole e immagini!

WOLF

THE THIRD LITTLE PIG

THE FIRST LITTLE PIG

THE SECOND LITTLE PIG

A Crossword

Risolvi il cruciverba illustrato!

A Maze

Help the third little Pig to escape from the wolf!

Aiuta il terzo Porcellino a scappare dal Lupo!

A little dictionary

••• **sostantivi** •••

BRICK: MATTONE
CHIMNEY: CAMINO
DEN: TANA
END: FINE
FIREPLACE: CAMINETTO
HOUSE: CASA
LADDER: SCALA (A PIOLI)
MOTHER: MADRE
PIG: MAIALE
POT: PENTOLA
ROAD: STRADA
STICK: BASTONE, ASSICELLA DI LEGNO
STRAW: PAGLIA
WOLF: LUPO

••• **aggettivi** •••

ALONE: SOLO
ANGRY: ARRABBIATO
BAD: CATTIVO
BIG: GRANDE
HAPPY: FELICE
LITTLE: PICCOLO
POOR: POVERO

••• **verbi** •••

to **BLOW:** SOFFIARE
to **BUILD:** COSTRUIRE
to **BUY:** COMPRARE
to **EAT:** MANGIARE
to **GO:** ANDARE
to **HEAR:** SENTIRE
to **KNOW:** SAPERE, CONOSCERE
to **LEAVE:** LASCIARE, ANDARSENE
to **LET:** PERMETTERE, LASCIARE
to **LOCK:** CHIUDERE A CHIAVE
to **LOOK FOR:** CERCARE
to **MEET:** INCONTRARE
to **OPEN:** APRIRE
to **WALK:** CAMMINARE
to **WANT:** VOLERE
to **WORK:** LAVORARE

A cura di Margherita Giromini
Illustrazioni: Barbara Bongini
Progetto grafico
e impaginazione: Simonetta Zuddas

www.giunti.it

© 2008, 2016 Giunti Editore S.p.A.
Via Bolognese, 165 - 50139 Firenze - Italia
Piazza Virgilio, 4 - 20123 Milano - Italia

Prima edizione: marzo 2004

Prima edizione con CD allegato: settembre 2008
Seconda ristampa: ottobre 2018

Stampato presso Lito Terrazzi srl, stabilimento di Iolo